FINDING *Happiness*

DAY · by · DAY

Swami Kriyananda

Crystal Clarity Publishers, Nevada City, CA 95959
Copyright © 2013 Hansa Trust
All rights reserved. Published 2013

Printed in China.

ISBN-13: 978-1-56589-280-4
ePub ISBN: 978-1-56589-534-8

1 3 5 7 9 10 8 6 4 2

Cover design, interior design and layout by Tejindra Scott Tully

Photographs by Barbara Bingham

Library of Congress Cataloging-in-Publication Data

Kriyananda, Swami.
  Finding happiness : one day at a time / Swami Kriyananda. -- 1st [edition].
    pages cm
  Includes bibliographical references and index.
  ISBN 978-1-56589-280-4 (quality pbk. : alk. paper)
  ISBN 978-1-56589-534-8 (epub : alk. paper)
1. Spiritual life. 2. Happiness--Miscellanea. 3. Maxims. I. Title.

  BP605.S4K74 2013
  294.5'44--dc23

  2013018638

---

www.crystalclarity.com / 800.424.1055 — 530.478.7600

These sayings contain my sincere attempt
to inspire people — to inspire you, friend —
to find happiness, and to make your life that which,
in the depths of your heart, you know it can be.

SWAMI KRIYANANDA

Life can be a humdrum monotony of similar experiences. Days, months, even years go by, without any substantial change of circumstances or increase of fulfillment.

But here is a secret many people are discovering: When your thoughts become more positive and expansive, your life improves.

When you change from the inside, your whole world changes.

True happiness springs from within.

And there are ways, deliberate choices that make that happiness grow.

Therefore, this book of thoughts and actions for your to experiment with.

All of these suggestions, offered here by Swami Kriyananda, are based on universal principles that lead to inner happiness.

"I suggest you take one thought at a time from the following pages," Kriyananda writes. "Keep it before you throughout the day, as a reminder. Repeat it out loud, or mentally, letting it sink into your subconscious. And look for situations in your life to which you can apply it creatively."

May your practice of these principles in daily life be your secret key to finding happiness.

Joy to you,

Ananda Community

January

January 1 | LIVING JOYFULLY

There will never be another today.
Make the most of it.

January 2 | INNER FREEDOM

Live in your present commitments,
not in any regret for the past.

January 3 | EMOTIONAL HEALING

Practice the presence of God. Share with Him every thought, every feeling, every act.

January 4 | MAGNETIC COMMUNICATION

Smile with your eyes, not only with your lips.

January 5 | EMOTIONAL HEALING

Relinquish personal desire by relating your emotions to a broader arc of feeling: love for a friend, or the joy of feeling free from external circumstances, or respect for the right of others to make their own decisions and their own mistakes.

Accept others
as they are,
and you will
encounter friends
everywhere
you go.

January 7 | SPIRITUAL FRIENDSHIP

Include other people's happiness in your own.

•

January 8 | ETERNAL LOVE

Love is reverence—less for each other than for Love itself, the eternal gift of God, of Life.

•

January 9 | MAGNETIC COMMUNICATION

Present points of mutual agreement before proceeding to your central theme.

January 10 | INNER HAPPINESS

Happiness is a smile of comfort
to the sorrowful.

January 11 | SUCCESSFUL LIVING

Concentration is the key to success
in every undertaking.

January 12 | BRINGING PEACE TO EARTH

Calm the feelings in your own heart.

When speaking
with people, talk with
your eyes, not only
with words.
To look away is to don
a mental mask.

January 14 | SELF-ACCEPTANCE

Strive to serve others consciously, as an instrument of a Higher Power.

January 15 | RADIANT HEALTH AND WELL-BEING

Eat in a harmonious environment. Avoid eating where there is discord.

January 16 | INSPIRED LEADERSHIP

Listen to reason no matter who voices it. In every situation, try to sense what is really trying to happen.

January 17 | INNER PEACE

Inner peace is desirelessness.

January 18 | SPIRITUAL FRIENDSHIP

Don't ask more of others than
you would ask of yourself.

January 19 | SECRETS FOR WOMEN

A vortex of disturbed emotions is often
dissipated by a sense of humor and
a heartfelt laugh.

January 20 | SECRETS FOR MEN

Place more reliance on the power of thought
than on physical strength.

January 21 | TRUE PROSPERITY

Hold positive expectations, supported by
a dynamic will.

January 22 | SUCCESSFUL LIVING

Before making any important decision in life,
consult your inner silence.

Nothing and nobody can affect who you are in your soul. In your interior castle, be ever secure and at peace.

What should you do when someone falsely accuses you? Try answering, "Now that you've reduced me to a level you can handle, maybe we can talk as friends."

When conversing with people, talk *with* them, not *at* them.

January 26 | INNER PEACE

Project peace outward into your environment.

January 27 |

Don't expect too much of others.
Thus we develop the capacity not to
expect too much of ourselves.

January 28 | EMOTIONAL HEALING

Keep a sense of humor, especially when
things turn out differently from the way
you hoped.

January 29 | SPIRITUAL FRIENDSHIP

No one, ever, could replace perfectly those
whose friendship you enjoy today. Make the
most of your present friendships.

Sit up straight; stand straight;
hold your shoulders back, your chest up,
your head high. Live more in the spine;
let your movements flow outward
from that inner center.

●

Don't allow your decisions
to be influenced by people's likes and
dislikes—especially your own.

February

February 1 | SUCCESSFUL LIVING

Concentrate single-mindedly on any task
you set yourself to.

February 2 | SUCCESSFUL LIVING

Constantly be willing to reevaluate
your first principles.

February 3 | INNER HAPPINESS

Give up personal attachments;
recognize that nothing and no one truly
belongs to us since all is God's.

•

February 4 | MAGNETIC COMMUNICATION

Remain calm under attack, withholding
recognition from comments that are made
simply to offend.

•

February 5 | COMFORT AND JOY

Do one thing *today* to bring solace to another
who is grieving. Offer yourself inwardly as a
channel for Divine Solace.

Have the patience to adjust every plan of action to objective reality.

Pay more attention to the tone of your voice. Magnetize that tone by lifting it up from the heart, then releasing it to soar out through the forehead. Keep the vocal cords relaxed. Your voice will be a delight to listen to if you can express through it calm heart-feeling.

February 8 | SPIRITUAL FRIENDSHIP

Never belittle a friend's enthusiasm.

February 9 | CREATING HARMONY

Forgive others, and Life itself will forgive you many wrongs you have done.

February 10 | EMOTIONAL HEALING

The secret of overcoming depression is useful activity, selflessly devoted to the welfare of others.

February 11 | BRINGING PEACE TO EARTH

Touch others daily with the wand of inner peace.

February 12 | MAGNETIC COMMUNICATION

Spend more time in listening to others. To speak excessively is anesthetizing.

A person reveals his own character
by the things he approves of
or disapproves of in others.
What you criticize in others is what
you harbor in yourself.

Speak more with your eyes,
the windows of the soul.
By using your eyes when you speak,
it will be as if those windows
were framed with
colorful curtains, making the home
warm and inviting.

If someone tells lies against you, say to him, "You've missed the mark this time, but keep trying. Who among us is perfect? With a little patience, I don't doubt you'll find something I've done wrong."

What is the greatest panacea? Love!

Temper the sword of reason in the fire of practicality. Ask of any idea not merely that it be reasonable, but that it work.

Give others credit,
where possible,
in the anecdotes
you tell.

Live a healthy life: exercise regularly,
eat properly, breathe deeply.

Leadership is enthusiasm! Win others
to an idea by the joy you feel in it.

When walking, breathe deeply and
rhythmically: Inhale counting four, hold four,
exhale four, hold four. Repeat this exercise
six to twelve times. Make it a point to
breathe from the diaphragm.

Light a candle of kindness in your heart
whenever you feel a need to correct
someone. Hold it there unwaveringly.

Be solution-oriented, not
problem-oriented—having faith
that within every problem there
lies an inherent solution.

Don't substitute self-blame
for self-correction.

February 25 | MAGNETIC COMMUNICATION

Make positive suggestions, not negative ones.

February 26 | BRINGING PEACE TO EARTH

Live less at your periphery, and more at your heart-center.

February 27 | INNER HAPPINESS

Happiness is being grateful for the hurts
one receives, recognizing them as channels
of understanding and wisdom.

February 28 | WINNING PEOPLE TO YOUR IDEAS

Concentrate as much on the other person's
needs as on your own.

February 29 | COMFORT AND JOY

Pray today for someone who considers
himself your enemy. Tell him mentally
that you are his friend.

March

March 1 | SUCCESSFUL LIVING

See your work primarily as a service to others, not as a means to personal gain.

●

March 2 | SPIRITUAL FRIENDSHIP

Don't criticize.
Sincerely voice beneficial truths.

Prefer the truth to mere opinions—even if
the opinions are your own.

Tell your detractors, "You help me when you
speak against me, by giving me an opportunity
to affirm the inward nature of true joy.
Thank you, friend. I wish you only well."

Watch yourself as though through the eyes
of another person. Do you like what you see?
If not, then change yourself.

The secret of aging gracefully
is to welcome with a fresh, creative spirit
every new experience.

Envy no one. View the successes and failures
of others empathetically as your own.

Accept criticism impersonally, without
thinking who has offered it, or to whom
it has been offered. The only issue, really,
is whether the criticism is just.

Be always even-minded
and cheerful. To rise and fall
with the waves of emotion
is to sacrifice mental clarity
for confusion.

March 10 |

Inner peace is willingness. Learn to say Yes when your mental habits, born of negativity and laziness, urge you to cry No!

March 11 | SUCCESSFUL LIVING

Do willingly whatever needs to be done.

March 12 | RADIANT HEALTH AND WELL-BEING

Exercise. Be conscious of the life-force flowing in every movement.

Success is meeting every challenge
from your calm center within.
Seek strength and guidance intuitively,
in your inner self.

Raise your level of energy.
Exercise vigorously every day.
Breathe deeply. Sit and stand erect.
Eat properly—a preponderance of
fresh fruits and vegetables, less meat.
A healthy body filled with vitality
makes for healthy mental attitudes.

Identify yourself with
your high potential, not
with your mistakes.
To identify yourself with
weakness, even in
the name of self-honesty,
is to accept weakness
as your reality.

You can help bring peace on earth by thinking *peace* whenever you look into people's eyes.

When tempted to lament any circumstance, ask yourself, "How am I likely to feel a week from now? A month? A year?" Sooner or later you'll stop feeling bad. Why waste all that time? Be happy now!

Listen to yourself. Do you like what you hear? Just as the eyes are the windows of the soul, so is the voice its clear echo.

Under-emphasize the pronoun "I."

Speak the truth impersonally, but at the same time kindly. For no matter how unwelcome a truth, its effect, if people accept it, is always beneficial.

Don't seek merely emotional joy. The emotions fluctuate. Seek joy, rather, in the calmness at the center of every emotion. As the Bible says: "Comfort ye your hearts."

Whenever you feel inspired to make suggestions, concentrate not on your own need to make them, but on the other person's need to hear. Wait even then—for months, if need be—until you perceive in your partner a *readiness* to hear what you have to say.

There is no adversity so great that it cannot be turned to advantage.

Support a friend in truth, even if it means confessing your own error.

Accept reality as it is. Expect nothing of others, and their words and actions will find you always inwardly at peace.

March 26 | INNER FREEDOM

Life is compromise. Make sure only that you adjust your compromises to your principles, and not your principles to any convenient compromise.

March 27 | MAGNETIC COMMUNICATION

Relax your voice if you would put warmth into it. Speak from the heart, rather than (thinly) from the throat and vocal cords.

Wise is he who disapproves of nothing, who judges no one but accepts everything as a necessary part of the cosmic drama.

Refrain from making leaps of logic for which your listeners may not be prepared.

Accommodate your ideas to those
of others if you want those persons
to carry them out. How much, really,
does it matter who gets the credit?

March 31 | RADIANT HEALTH AND WELL-BEING

The secret of radiant health and well-being
is inner happiness, radiated outward
in a sense of well-being to others.
Happiness is the fruit of faith in life, in God,
in one's own high potential.

April

April 1 | MAGNETIC COMMUNICATION

Listen for the thoughts and vibrations
behind people's words.

April 2 | SUCCESSFUL LIVING

If you have a good idea, welcome
suggestions for its improvement but
let no one diffuse or dilute it.

View your problems
as though from
the mountain heights—
that is to say,
with detachment.
Any view of them
from the proximity of
personal involvement
will be distorted.

Inner peace is daily meditation, tapping
the wellspring of soul-peace within you.

View every action as a path
to some greater good.

Try to appreciate others' opinions,
even when you don't agree with them.
Mutual appreciation is a bridge that spans
the chasm of miscommunication.

Eat more fresh, raw foods,
fewer that have been cooked,
and none that are stale
or over-cooked. Remember,
your food consists of more
than chemicals. Choose foods
that are rich in life-force.

Take responsibility for your life, for
nothing happens without a cause that
can be traced, usually, to some attitude,
some expectation—perhaps held only
subconsciously—in yourself.

Be generous in victory, calmly accepting
in defeat. Calm acceptance is itself
a form of victory.

Realize that your own peace has
its source not in you, but in Infinity.

Laugh from your heart, not only
from your intellect.

Face your trials in life cheerfully.
Don't hide from them, for life's trials
are like dogs: They lose heart
if you confront them, but give
eager chase if you flee.

April 13 | SECRETS FOR WOMEN

To overcome a tendency to take things
too personally, refer the remarks of others
to impersonal principles. If, for example,
someone exclaims, "People are such liars!"
emphasize the principle of truthfulness over
people's inability to live by that principle.

Talk in order to give
utterance to thought, and not
simply to make noise.

Share your own greater
knowledge or experience.
Let crystal clarity
be your guide.

Develop intuitive reasoning by feeling
in your heart whether your premise is
correct or incorrect. To arrive at the truth
in such matters, remove yourself a little
from the opinions of others.

If you make a practice of counting to ten
when you are angry, visualize each number
as a stage in the progressive expansion
of your consciousness. Add to that
expansion, if possible, the dimension of
growing sympathy.

April 18 | TRUE PROSPERITY

Prosperity is a mind-set
of inventiveness. Success in
any field demands a
creative outlook, similar to
that of an artist.

April 19 | ETERNAL LOVE

Love is stillness. Only in stillness
can love attain perfection.
For love is not passion; human love
is a reflection of divine love.
And God is perfect stillness.

Don't allow yourself to feel that you deserve more of life than you are receiving. What life metes out to you is exactly what you have earned from it.

If someone speaks against you, say to him, "Thank you. Only a friend would try to improve me at the cost of his inner peace."

Have the courage to make clear decisions.
Don't let "What if?" and "What if not?"
keep you sitting on a fence.
Say "Yes" or "No," not "Maybe."

April 23 | SPIRITUAL FRIENDSHIP

Seek transcendence in your relationships.
Love your friends for their high potentials.

April 24 | CREATING HARMONY

Strive to be a healing influence always,
on both yourself and others.

Concentrate on the vital essence of what you eat. The more you make it a practice to eat consciously, the more the energy in what you eat will fill your being—and the more, as a result, you will *want* to eat correctly.

Learn the art of brevity. A single sentence may be long remembered, whereas lengthy discourses are usually soon forgotten.

While it is conducive to mental clarity to distance yourself a little from your problems, don't withhold your sympathies from the problems of others.

Inner peace is loving God.
Strive always to be worthy of
God's love for you. He is
Heavenly Father, Divine Mother,
Eternal Beloved, Friend.

April 29 | INSPIRED LEADERSHIP

Put your heart into everything you do.
Don't give projects merely endorsement.

April 30 | SELF-ACCEPTANCE

To laugh when others tease you is self-
acceptance. Thus you remove any subtle
sting that their words might contain.

May 1 | RADIANT HEALTH AND WELL-BEING

Be more conscious
of sounds, especially of music.
For music, whether calming
or discordant, cheerful or
depressing, affects the entire
nervous system. It can make
a person vital and responsive,
or lifeless and resentful.

May 2 | SUCCESSFUL LIVING

If you have a good idea, stand up for it.
Be loyal to it, as you'd be loyal to a friend.
Let no wave of deprecation
deflect it from its course.

May 3 | LIVING JOYFULLY

Pay special attention to those whom habit
has conditioned you to consider a bit foolish.
From judgmental attitudes issue
many of our worst mistakes.

May 4 | BRINGING PEACE TO EARTH

You will help to bring peace on earth
if you never try to make peace at the
cost of high and noble principles.

To express your thoughts more interestingly,
put melody in your voice.

Learn to say "*Yes!*" instantly, whenever
your impulse is to grumble or cry "No!"
Welcome life in all its variety and challenges.
Keep your heart open, like the petals
of a daisy, to life's experiences.
Overcome the tendency to withdraw
into yourself in a spirit of rejection.

If someone criticizes you, say, "Thank you for your suggestion. I will think about it." In that way you don't say that you agree with him, but only that you have heard him with an open mind.

Don't conceal whatever counter arguments
there may be, but present those
arguments fairly, then place them in
a broader, truer context.

Make contentment your
criterion of prosperity.

To be a peace-maker; be peaceful, first,
in your own heart.

Love omnipresent God in each other.
Thus will you always feel
drawn to the divine perfection
behind the human mask.
For humanity struggles—in the face
of countless obstacles, and by
many and various routes—
toward ideals that are eternal.

See divine love behind
the blessing of friendship.

May 13 | SUCCESSFUL LIVING

Don't complain at perceived misfortune. Whining only tests other people's patience. Courage in the face of adversity, on the other hand, wins universal admiration.

May 14 | COMFORT AND JOY

See joy as the fruit of inner peace, not of noise and excitement.

Maintain a sense of perspective.
Obsessions only narrow the mind.

Choose your words kindly if you
would invite understanding.

When someone points out to you a mistake
you committed, and you recognize that he
is right, don't blame yourself. Be grateful,
rather, that now you can work to
remove an impediment to your happiness.
The impediment was there anyway;
to recognize it is your good fortune.

Affirm good health and mental peace even
in the face of illness and disappointment.
When your light shines brightly from within,
illness will shut its eyes tightly and run away.

May 19 | SELF-ACCEPTANCE

Be grateful for the tests you attract in life.
Recognize them as necessary to your growth
in strength and wisdom.

May 20 | INNER HAPPINESS

Laugh with your whole being, not only
with your vocal cords.

Pay more attention to the words of children.
They often express the simple clarity
of wisdom.

Compete against yourself in life's race.
Be less concerned with competing
against others.

One secret of attaining inner freedom is
mentally to cast into the wind every dry
straw of desire and attachment.

May 24 | MAGNETIC COMMUNICATION

Choose your words for clarity.
Don't expect your listeners
to do the editing for you.

May 25 | WINNING PEOPLE TO YOUR IDEAS

Forge lasting, not brittle, bonds,
lest you sacrifice their loyalty
and high esteem.

May 26 | INNER HAPPINESS

Offer hope to those
who have lost hope.

Don't drive people—
inspire them.

Let your reason be guided
by calm, intuitive feeling,
never by the turbulence
of emotions.

Show respect for others, and they
will always respect you.

Seek peace at that calm center within you
where nothing can touch you: neither fire, nor
flood, nor loss of any kind—not even death.

What is the point of courting admiration?
You aren't central in any universe
but your own. What others praise today,
they may reject tomorrow. Seek rather
to shine before your own conscience.

June

June 1 | INNER FREEDOM

Live fully NOW, if you would
develop golden memories.

●

June 2 | MAGNETIC COMMUNICATION

Think *space* in your speech.
Try not to crowd your ideas.

Seek variety in your life together;
never letting routine chords
dull the melody of your romance.

To transmute sexual energy, feel
it flowing constantly up the spine
from the base to the brain.
Much joy attends this practice.

Truth need not be shouted, unless,
perhaps, to make it audible to a crowd.
Truth should be stated sensitively.
Usually, therefore, it should be understated.

Give of yourself freely, and don't think
about what others may give you in return.
Impersonality is the secret of true generosity.

Offer happiness to the sorrowful.

Never place expediency above truth.

●

Treat the world as a friend and
it will *be* your friend.

●

The center of the universe,
as far as your perceptions are concerned,
lies in yourself. Never belittle your potential,
for everything you can ever know
begins with self-acceptance and
develops through self-understanding.

To slice through the confusion that
words so often cause, send out
mental tendrils as if to sense ideas
before they are even expressed.

Imagine yourself always surrounded by light.
Absorb this light into yourself. Expand it
consciously. Include in it the people around
you, the very space in which you live.

Encourage good ideas
no matter what their source.

Think of the climb up life's mountain
not as a trial, but as an ascent to victory.

Nonattachment is not indifference.
Be deeply concerned always to find right
and true solutions to life's problems.

How you react to people
and to circumstances is *your* choice
and no one else's. Let no one force
reactions from you that are incompatible
with your own inner peace.

Recognize greed and envy as the
offspring, not the parents, of
discontent. Cultivate harmonious
feelings in the heart. Affirm:
"I am complete in myself.
I am whole! I accept
whatever comes of itself,
while doing my best always to
achieve my valid goals."

When troubles beset you, seek both
their cause and their solution in yourself.
Never accept for yourself the victim's role.

June 19 | INNER PEACE

Work cooperatively *with* others,
rather than competitively against them.

June 20 | INSPIRED LEADERSHIP

Support enthusiasm in others.

Vigorously meet your challenges.
Don't dilute your present energy by
dwelling at length on past victories.

The gift of kind words can be more
precious than any mundane good.

Be loyal to others, and they'll be loyal to you.

Be impartial in your use of
reasoning. Don't use it to win,
but to reveal the truth.

The secret of success, and indeed
of genius, is to pay keen attention
to detail without ever sacrificing
the broader view.

June 26 | EMOTIONAL HEALING

Visualize yourself as seated at
the heart of infinity. For the universe,
as far as your own awareness of it
is concerned, is centered in *you*.
If you send forth rays of faith and
good will to all, life will sustain you
through every difficulty.

June 27 | ETERNAL LOVE

Love is adaptability.
Keep your love fluid, so that
it may fill every vessel that
life places before you.

Before speaking, weigh your words—
but not too heavily.

To overcome worry, live more in
the moment. Leave future problems
to be resolved by future energy.

To proclaim your opinions too loudly
is to call more attention to yourself
than to your opinions.

July

July 1 | SPIRITUAL FRIENDSHIP

Whatever you want from others
—love, support, loyalty—
you be the first to give.

July 2 | LIVING JOYFULLY

A stranger is no stranger
if you can make him smile.

Nonattachment bestows inner peace, which is the precursor of contentment. It fosters relaxation, the companion of good health.

●

Work with others' strengths; don't belittle others for their weaknesses.

●

Be happy in yourself, not in the outer circumstances of your life.

Give more thought to
communion with others than to
communication with them.

Develop gracefulness
of movement, that you may
keep your thoughts fluid.

When tempted to feel agitated,
relax your heart. It is there, in the heart,
that both calmness and excitement
have their beginning.

You have within you the strength
to conquer every adversity.

Reduce the number of your likes and dislikes.
Find contentment within yourself,
and in the lasting blessing of true friends.

July 11 | SECRETS FOR MEN

Don't be afraid to follow your own star,
though it shine for no one else.

July 12 | TRUE PROSPERITY

Make time for singing.
What is prosperity, after all,
if in striving for it one loses
the capacity to enjoy life?

July 13 | SPIRITUAL FRIENDSHIP

Give others the respect
that allows them to make
their own mistakes.

Realize that you are
an integral part of everything
that is, sustained by
the Power that brought the
very universe into existence.
Open your heart to life!
Cease to see yourself
as a lonely plant, waterless
on an empty desert.

Be willing on occasion to give others
the last word.

Look to the past as a guideline to
improving the future, but seek perfection
beyond time, in the eternal NOW.

Be truthful always. Wisely has it been said,
"Where there is truth, there is victory."

Cultivate happy memories—in others
as well as in yourself. Make a practice
of asking people, "What has been
the best day of your life?"

Think, when you hear a bird singing,
that its song expresses Nature's joy.
Bring that joy into your own heart
for you, too, are a child of Nature.

Live *today*. To live in any other time frame is
to wander in a vague world of dreams.

See divine love behind every
trial in life. Remember also:
Only in combat do warriors
become strong.

Welcome challenges
and you will find them working
with you, not against you.

Today, tell someone to whom you're close,
"I appreciate you for what you *are*."

July 24 | MAGNETIC COMMUNICATION

Say what you mean, and mean what you say.
Infuse energy into every word you speak.

●

July 25 | INNER PEACE

Live more at the pause between
two activities.

●

July 26 | SELF-ACCEPTANCE

Seek the approval of people whose
opinions you respect.

Concentrate on others'
virtues, not on their faults.

Happiness is seeing one's
work as service.

Let everything you do be
dynamic to your consciousness.
To live automatically is to slip
backward on the scale of evolution.

Go out of your way to show respect
to those who are ignored by others.

Don't think of problems in terms
of the difficulties they present.
View them, rather, as opportunities.

August

August 1 | LIVING JOYFULLY

Tell a story today to bring a smile to the face
of someone who is sad or depressed.

August 2 | SUCCESSFUL LIVING

Hold cheerful expectations of life.
The quality of energy you put forth
determines what you get back.

Uplift moods by
focusing their energy
at a point midway
between the eyebrows—
the seat of superconscious
awareness in the body.

August 4 | SPIRITUAL FRIENDSHIP

Look upon members of the other sex
as neither prey nor predators, but as friends.
For as you treat them, so, almost always,
will they treat you.

●

August 5 | MAGNETIC COMMUNICATION

Speak courteously to your own nearest
and dearest. Courtesy is the oil
that keeps the wheels of love and
friendship turning smoothly.

●

August 6 | SECRETS FOR MEN

To develop self-respect, develop
respect for others.

Project every movement
outward from your heart
like a wave of energy.

See no one as a stranger.

Accept praise with good humor
and a grain of salt.
What you receive today may be
withdrawn tomorrow.

August 10 | SUCCESSFUL LIVING

Act from your center; don't *react*
at your periphery.

August 11 | SECRETS FOR WOMEN

When people hurt you, heal the sickness of
their disharmony by offering them kindness,
understanding, and forgiveness.

August 12 | INNER FREEDOM

Most pain is a matter of acceptance.
Cease defining it as pain, and you will
perceive it as merely a sensation—not as
something from which to cringe.

Make helpful suggestions,
but refrain from criticizing.

Respond with courtesy when people are discourteous to you. Their rudeness is their problem, not yours. Courtesy, on the other hand, will often act as a soothing balm upon their troubled feelings.

Water the flowers.
Water the hearts of others.

Treat others as though you
were *treating* them.

August 17 | SELF-ACCEPTANCE

Stand straight and tall.
As a child of God you are
the equal of anyone on earth.
Humility is self-honesty,
but not self-deprecation.

Uplift moods of depression on wings of song.
Soar up mentally into the sky with
the flight of birds.

•

Allow nothing to force your hand until
you first affirm, "Whatever my response,
it will be of my own choosing and
not imposed upon me."

•

Grant other people the right to their own
opinions, and you'll find yourselves in
agreement on most issues.

Eat to nourish your body rather
than simply for pleasure. Chew your food
carefully; draw energy from it.
Eat consciously, not absent-mindedly.
Eat cheerfully, drawing from
your food its subtlest essence in
the form of consciousness.

August 22 | INNER HAPPINESS

Offer encouragement where
you see discouragement.

August 23 | SUCCESSFUL LIVING

Make sure you will do something
before you announce that you'll do it.
Be true to your word.

Think of every flower
as calling to you.
If you would
become beautiful,
contemplate beauty
in the world
around you.

Work with your strengths.
Don't struggle unprofitably
with your weaknesses.
For the stronger you become
in yourself, the weaker will be
the grip of those weaknesses
on your mind.

Kind sentiment, if it lacks
the support of kind deeds, is not
true friendship. Friendship is
much more than a smile.

Overcome anger by broadening your emotional base. Reflect, so what seems upsetting to you today may appear in a completely new light tomorrow.

Love people—if not for themselves, then simply for the joy you find in loving.

Disarm critics by saying to them, "I see and appreciate your point of view. Now, may I offer an alternate one?"

Think well of people, in your heart.
For all of us are fellow travelers in the desert.
We need cooperation, friendship,
and support from one another.

Behold a river, and think of it as the flow
of your own thoughts. Affirm your mind's
ability to adapt, like flowing water,
to new situations and ideas.

September

September 1 | LIVING JOYFULLY

Watch the play of children.
Study their absorption in the moment.

●

September 2 | RADIANT HEALTH AND WELL-BEING

To balance your diet,
eat food of different colors.

Be humble but not abject.
Humility is self-forgetfulness
in the contemplation
of greater realities.

If you keep your mind open to opportunity,
opportunity will find its way to your door.

Put bright colors in your surroundings
as a means of affirming
brightness in your own life.

September 6 | SECRETS FOR MEN

Expand the love you feel for your own
to include all beings as your own.

•

September 7 | SUCCESSFUL LIVING

Be more concerned with what *is*
than with what you'd like things to be.

•

September 8 | LIVING JOYFULLY

If you want to enjoy life, take yourself
a little less seriously.

Stand by your
perceptions of truth,
by your own strengths,
by your own inner guidance.
Don't make crutches
of other people.

Overcome anger by recognizing that yours is not the only view of reality. Others may see things very differently from you, yet just as validly.

⬤

Show your appreciation to others for what they are and for what they do. A spirit of gratitude opens the door to life's abundance.

⬤

Think of something you fear to lose, then ask yourself, "Would I not be just the same person, if I lost it, as I am right now?"

Try to understand different points of view
from your own, for the mind resembles
the body in this important respect:
Unless you stretch it to keep it limber;
it will ossify.

Live *in*, but not *for*, the present moment.

Support others in their worthwhile goals,
and let them *feel* your support. Don't merely
wave your abstract blessings.

The world mirrors back to you
your wisdom, or your folly.
If you don't like what you see in
the world around you, think first,
"How can I change myself?"

Give others their due,
but be generous also in allowing
them to give you yours.

To overcome the temptation to tell tales
on others, tell good ones on yourself.

Show respect for convention,
but remember that conventions were
created first by unconventional people.

With every breath you take,
inhale energy. *Feel* the energy
filling your body, from your toes
to the very top of your head.

September 21 |

Don't impose your ideas on others.
Offer them.

●

September 22 | SELF-ACCEPTANCE

Be dignified but not proud.
Live in recognition of the divine power
within you to accomplish all things.

●

September 23 | INNER HAPPINESS

Seek freedom within yourself—the freedom
that is your inalienable soul-right.

Think of those material things
to which you are emotionally attached,
then cast them mentally into a great fire.
Affirm joyously, "In my heart
I am forever free."

Be good-humored about the shortcomings
of others, and you'll find it easier to face
your own shortcomings. Remember,
your faults are as gigantic or as tiny
as your imagination makes them.

September 26 | SUCCESSFUL LIVING

When you decide to do something,
back it with the full power of your will.

●

September 27 | SPIRITUAL FRIENDSHIP

Sow seeds of faith where
others have sown doubt.

●

September 28 | EMOTIONAL HEALING

To overcome anger, place a
higher priority on good will.

When talking to people,
try to tune in to their reality.
Although it may be very different
from your own, communication
across a chasm is rarely effective.

Don't think, "How can I do this
differently?" Don't even think,
"How can I do it better?"
Think, "How should it be done?"

October

October 1 | INNER PEACE

Move consciously in an
aura of peace.

●

October 2 | BRINGING PEACE TO EARTH

Live by the spirit—not by the
mere letter, of God's law.

Soul-memory is wisdom.
Develop the power of memory
by concentrating single-mindedly
on everything you do.

Don't close your heart when hurt.
To do so is to suffer twice.

Be more concerned with
the truth of a situation than with
how it looks to others.

Laugh at
others' jokes
as though
you'd be delighted
to have told
them yourself.

Possess things as necessary, but let
no thing possess you.

If you decide to defend a principle, see joy
as the underlying reality of your defense.
Fight to win, but not to destroy.

To bring abundance into your life,
see money as a flow of energy,
not as a static quantity.

October 10 | RADIANT HEALTH AND WELL-BEING

Eat light foods to offset the heavy ones.
Drink more liquids—at least
two quarts every day.

October 11 | SELF-ACCEPTANCE

Be matter-of-fact about your
accomplishments, but proud of the
accomplishments of others.

October 12 | LIVING JOYFULLY

To develop will power, concentrate
your forces; don't scatter them.

Be not afraid to dream greatness.
Courage is the secret of every
worthwhile accomplishment.

Correct others by your example,
not by nagging criticism.

Give others freedom to be themselves.
Appreciate the differences between
their ways and yours.

Feminine qualities are as strong,
in their own way, as those that are
more notably masculine. Air and water
are as powerful as fire. Patient endurance,
receptivity, and the ability to adapt to
circumstances can ensure victory where
aggressiveness crashes in defeat.

Be aware of your mental process as you
enjoy things, lest you become possessed
by them instead of self-possessed.
Never allow your center to shift away
from the Self within.

In yourself lies the only
key to happiness there is.
Think of things, people,
or circumstances that seem,
to your mind, to make
you happy, and visualize them
as so many mirrors,
merely reflecting back
to you your eager
expectations of them.

Why compare yourself with others?
When driving on the freeway, there will be
cars ahead of you and many more behind.
Keep your mind serenely focused on
your own destination.

To be creative, relax mentally; let creativity
pass through you, as a flow of intuition.

Be more concerned with understanding
others than with being understood by them.

They too, then, will be more concerned
with understanding you.

October 22 | SUCCESSFUL LIVING

Be a student of life.
Even if you teach, do so
in the thought that you, too,
are just a student sharing
priceless discoveries.

October 23 | EMOTIONAL HEALING

For yourself, try always to keep
a sense of humor. Be generous, however.
Don't bludgeon people with your good
humor if they aren't receptive to it.

Don't joke too much.
Show people that
your friendship for them
is a serious
heart-commitment.

Develop a sense of community with others.
See that community as consisting of more
than your little family, more than your
neighborhood, more than the town or city
in which you live. Expand your sense
of community to include, finally,
the entire world.

Direct energy into the things you do.
Energy has its own intelligence.
It will make things happen for you
even if you didn't plan them.

October 27 |

Defuse criticism by saying, if possible,
"I agree with you. Let's work together
toward a workable solution."

October 28 | SUCCESSFUL LIVING

If you don't like what you see in life,
try changing your angle of vision.

October 29 | ETERNAL LOVE

Be not afraid to love. Even when love is
not requited, you will be forever richer
for having loved.

See divine love
behind the gift of human love.

When giving to others, give not only
what you think they would enjoy having,
but what *you* would enjoy giving them.

November

November 1 | INNER HAPPINESS

Accept whatever comes with an attitude
of calm inner freedom.

November 2 | INNER PEACE

Listen to melodies that uplift the heart
and fill it with enthusiasm and joy.
Shun as poison those melodies that make
the heart restless, angry, or indifferent.

Don't lose sight of your goal,
but at the same time concentrate
on winning present battles.
The war will then take care of itself.

Judge no one.
Who knows what hardships
others have suffered?

Devote more time to serious thought.
Ask yourself, "Am I doing
the best I can with my life?"

Invite others' questions and suggestions.
Don't simply announce your decisions.

●

Keep your energy flowing upward. Try this
exercise: Bend forward, exhaling: then inhale
slowly, straightening up, and raise your arms
high above the head; feel life vitalizing your
upper body all the way to the fingertips.

●

To develop concentration, do one thing
at a time, and do it well.

Be fair when conversing
with others. Try to understand
and appreciate their point
of view. Indeed, only through
understanding is there a hope
of influencing anyone.
Remember, truth is ultimately
what counts, not opinions.

Encourage a child, and you'll encourage
the development of your own high potentials.

Explore the relationships, more than
the differences, between other people's
ideas and your own.

Others may see you as their enemy.
Resolve, on your part, to be their friend.

Project your vibrations into those with whom you are speaking, that your communication may be more complete.

Greet everyone as a dear friend.

Trust Life, not people. Human nature is untrustworthy, whereas Life is obedient to unchanging laws.

Overcome the fear of death.
Deepen your awareness of the
central part in your being that
never changes, but that weaves
like a thread through life's tapestry.
The consciousness of change
is allied to the fear of death.
To see changelessness at the
heart of change, then,
is the secret of immortality.

Meet anger with silence,
respectfully, and for lack of fuel
the fires of anger will subside.

See yourself as a cause, not as an effect.
Accept from others only what you
choose to accept: their good suggestions
but not their insistence on them; their
constructive criticisms but not their anger.
Radiate into the world around you
the light of faith and wisdom.

Enlist support for your ideas; don't browbeat your coworkers with them.

⬤

View your lot in life, no matter how difficult, as a gift, not a misfortune. For not only is it what you've attracted and therefore earned, but you will find your growth only through acceptance of it.

⬤

Take the time to *listen* to the silence in the universe, within and around you.

November 22 | MAGNETIC COMMUNICATION

Defuse criticism by saying, "Thank you.
I appreciate your telling me how you feel."

November 23 | LIVING JOYFULLY

Trees can give you strength
if you see in them a reminder
of your own strength.

November 24 | BRINGING PEACE TO EARTH

Place more faith in divine
than in human law.

Happiness is doing joyfully and willingly
whatever needs to be done.

When dealing with others, actively seek
the highest good for both of you.
They too, then, will be more inclined
to think in terms of giving rather than taking.

Live to serve others rather than to benefit
from them. The more of yourself you can
relinquish in joyous service, the freer
you will discover yourself to be.

Wrap yourself in a
protective cloak of strength.
A strong will, wisely guided,
is the best shield
against adversity.

Overcome self-limiting attachments
by viewing them as prison bars.
Concentrate not on the bars themselves,
but on the space remaining
between them—space through which
you can escape to freedom.

Look upon members of the other sex
as *people*, not merely as "opposites."

December

December 1 | SPIRITUAL FRIENDSHIP

Treat your friends as though you still
had much to learn from them.

December 2 | CREATING HARMONY

In your efforts to improve your lot in life,
improve yourself. Strive always to become a
cause in life, not an effect.

Be decisive in thought.
Never tell yourself, merely,
"I'll try." Say, "I *will!*"

Judge no one, and others
of good will, will always
judge you kindly.

December 5 | INSPIRED LEADERSHIP

Give others credit wherever possible—
even, sometimes, when an idea
was first your own.

December 6 | RADIANT HEALTH AND WELL-BEING

Be a friend to all.

December 7 | LIVING JOYFULLY

This day will belong to you
if you greet it as a friend.

Happiness is relinquishing
the sense of "I" and "mine."

Live to share, not to hoard, and
you will always know abundance.

Think of the points on which
you and others are in agreement.
Don't concentrate so much
on points of disagreement.

December 11 | CREATING HARMONY

Include the success of others in your
dreams for your own success.

December 12 | MAGNETIC COMMUNICATION

Look for concrete examples to illustrate
your ideas. The more abstract a presentation,
the less others will welcome it as true.

December 13 | SUCCESSFUL LIVING

Use your judgment as you would a sword,
separating right from wrong, truth from error.
Slice through every trial and difficulty
with the blade of mental clarity.

Look upon members of both sexes as friends,
not as opponents on the battlefield of life.

December 15 | EMOTIONAL HEALING

As an aid to introspection, be more conscious
of the rhythms of your breath. In the breath
is reflected every fluctuation of feeling.

December 16 | INNER FREEDOM

To develop clarity of thought, be always
completely truthful with yourself.

Sit up straight. Gaze upward
frequently; try to keep your
awareness focused in the
frontal lobe of your brain,
at a point midway between
the eyebrows. Walk lightly.
Sit lightly. Smile often.

December 18 | INSPIRED LEADERSHIP

Hold your hand out to others.
Don't wait for them to come to you.

December 19 | MAGNETIC COMMUNICATION

Defuse criticism by saying, "Let's be friends
even if we can't always agree."

December 20 | SUCCESSFUL LIVING

Train your mind always to say "Yes" to life!

Happiness is not a brilliant climax
to years of grim struggle and anxiety.
It is a long succession of little decisions
simply to be happy in the moment.

Walk *consciously*. Live more
at your inner center, in the spine.
When walking, be conscious of
the energy moving through
your body.

To live simply is to breathe
the air of inner freedom.
Why suffocate yourself
in the crowded room of
useless possessions?

December 24 | SUCCESSFUL LIVING

Fight for the truth, not for self-interest, and you will always achieve victory in the end.

•

December 25 | EMOTIONAL HEALING

Whenever negative moods attack you,
put them into a broader,
more objective sense of reality.

•

December 26 | MAGNETIC COMMUNICATION

Listen to the pauses in people's speech.
Often, that's where the message is.

December 27 | ETERNAL LOVE

Be more concerned with how
you feel toward others than with
how they feel toward you.

●

December 28 | MAGNETIC COMMUNICATION

Speak courteously to strangers.
They are your own self in new, though
perhaps unexpected, forms.

●

December 29 | CREATING HARMONY

Love others as aspects of your own
expanded Self.

If you can forgive someone toward whom you've been holding a grudge, you will catch at least a glimpse of what it means to be truly free.

Make everyone you meet feel that he or she is in some way special to you.

*Crystal Clarity Publications has many
offerings to help you Find Happiness*

[
COMMUNITIES

YOGA & MEDITATION

EDUCATION *for* LIFE

HEALTHY FOODS

ENVIRONMENT & GARDENS
]

For more, please visit us at www.crystalclarity.com

CITIES OF LIGHT
What Communities Can Accomplish in the New Age
Swami Kriyananda (J. Donald Walters)

Cities of Light contains the positive, life-changing lessons and advice earned over the last 30 years at Ananda, a highly successful network of ten intentional communities on three continents. It explains how people everywhere, living in all kinds of communities—intentional or otherwise—can come together to build or improve their own communities, making them a haven for successful businesses, joy-filled interpersonal relationships, enlightened government, progressive education, and inspiring culture and the arts.

HOPE FOR A BETTER WORLD!
The Small Communities Solution
Swami Kriyananda (J. Donald Walters)

In these turbulent times when wars, religious strife, stifling bureaucracy, and urban decay threaten our very humanity, a fresh approach to the creation of a truly viable society is desperately needed. In this intellectual tour de force, Swami Kriyananda analyzes with deep insight the views expressed by many of the great thinkers in the West, including Plato, Copernicus, Machiavelli, Malthus, Adam Smith, Charles Darwin, Karl Marx, and Sigmund Freud. He studies their conceptions and misconceptions about the individual's relation to himself and to society. He shows where their influence has proved adverse, then offers deeply considered, fresh alternatives. Kriyananda urges the reader to resist the hypnosis of "intellectual authority." Seek the key to a happy and fulfilled life, he says, in personal integrity.

GOOD MORNING, GREAT SOULS
Transformations in Community
Gyandevi Fuller (Editor)

The photographs, conversations, stories, and informal talks in this book chronicle some of the small and great steps taken over the years by people from around the world who are walking the path of Self-realization at Ananda Village, in Northern California. Over the years, we have learned that focusing on helping each other to develop our inner lives, though it takes a great deal of energy and determination, is the key to living in harmony and brotherhood, and resembles a much larger version of the extended family, with all the responsibilities, rewards, and challenges implied.

THE ART & SCIENCE OF RAJA YOGA
Swami Kriyananda

This is the most comprehensive course on yoga and meditation available today, giving you a profound and intimate understanding of how to apply these age-old teachings, on a practical, as well as a spiritual, day-to-day level in this modern age. Over 450 pages of text and photos give you a complete and detailed presentation of hatha yoga (yoga postures), yoga philosophy, affirmations, meditation instruction, diet, and breathing techniques. Apply these teachings and techniques in your daily life and you will attain your highest soul potential: true happiness, inner peace, and the dynamic joy of your being.

SPIRITUAL YOGA
Awakening to Higher Awareness
Gyandev McCord

Imagine that you've hired Michelangelo to repaint your kitchen cabinets. Plain white. No doubt he would do a great job, but might you be missing out on something much better? It's the same with hatha yoga, which is above all a tool for spiritual growth. Many practitioners are missing its higher purpose: to help you raise your consciousness and achieve ever-greater happiness.

Based on the teachings of Paramhansa Yogananda, this wonderful book includes: the mind-energy-body connection; the art of meditation; spiritualizing yoga postures; spiritual yoga routines; affirmations and energy control suggestions; mastering pranayama (energy control); and breathing exercises for greater energy, calmness, and concentration.

ANANDA YOGA FOR HIGHER AWARENESS
Swami Kriyananda

This unique book teaches hatha yoga as it was originally intended: as a way to uplift your consciousness and aid your spiritual development. Kriyananda's inspiring affirmations and clearly written instructions show you how to attune yourself to the consciousness of each pose, so that each yoga posture becomes a doorway to life-affirming attitudes, clarity of understanding, and an increasingly centered and uplifted awareness. It includes standing poses, relaxation poses, spinal stretches, sitting poses, and inverted poses—all with photographs. With suggestions for routines of varying lengths for both beginning and advanced students.

HOW TO MEDITATE
A Step-by-Step Guide to the Art & Science of Meditation
Jyotish Novak

This clear and concise guidebook contains everything you need to start your practice. With easy-to-follow instructions, meditation teacher Jyotish Novak demystifies meditation—presenting the essential techniques so that you can quickly grasp them. Since it was first published in 1989, *How to Meditate* has helped thousands establish a regular meditation routine. This newly revised edition includes a bonus chapter on scientific studies showing the benefits of meditation, plus all-new photographs and illustrations.

"Meditation is a complicated term for something that is truly simple. *How To Meditate* is a guide to mastering meditation and reaping more of the benefit of the serenity of the matter. With tips on finding relaxation, opening your natural intuition, and more, this book is a must for those who want to unlock their spirituality." —*Midwest Book Review*

MEDITATION FOR STARTERS
Swami Kriyananda

Have you wanted to learn to meditate, but just never got around to it? Or tried "sitting in the silence" only to find yourself too restless to stay more than a few moments? If so, *Meditation for Starters* is just what you've been looking for—and with a companion CD, it provides everything you need to begin a meditation practice. Filled with easy-to-follow instructions, beautiful guided visualizations, and answers to important questions on meditation, this book includes: what meditation is (and isn't); how to relax your body and prepare yourself for going within; and techniques for interiorizing and focusing the mind.

LIVING WISELY, LIVING WELL
Swami Kriyananda

Want to transform your life? Tap into your highest potential? Get inspired, uplifted, and motivated?

This book contains 366 practical ways to improve your life—a thought for each day of the year. Each reading is warm with wisdom, alive with positive expectation, and provides simple actions that bring profound results. See life with new eyes. Discover hundreds of techniques for self-improvement.

EDUCATION FOR LIFE
Swami Kriyananda (J. Donald Walters)

Education for Life offers a constructive and brilliant alternative to what has been called the disaster of modern education. The need for a change is universally recognized. The statistics of illiteracy, drug abuse, and violence speak for themselves. In this book, Kriyananda traces the problems to an emphasis on technological competence at the expense of spiritual values, which alone can give higher meaning to life. *Education for Life* offers parents, educators, and concerned citizens everywhere techniques that are both compassionate and practical.

FOR GOODNESS' SAKE
Supporting Children & Teens in Discovering Life's Highest Values
Michael Nitai Deranja

Today's children need more than academic education—they also need positive values for making the most of their education and their lives. Selfishness, greed, and moodiness are common—but treatable!—burdens for many children. Michael Nitai Deranja offers simple-to-use, effective activities to help children learn—from their own experience—that expressing virtue actually brings them more happiness. Ages 4 to 17 will have fun with these activities as they explore seventeen different values, including cooperation, concentration, integrity, willingness, and many others. As children learn through direct, personal experience, these positive values become part of their lives.

I CAME FROM JOY!
Spiritual Affirmations and Activities for Children
Lorna Ann Knox

I Came From Joy! is a beautifully conceived, nonsectarian tool for developing a child's inner, spiritual life–ideal for parents, teachers, youth group leaders, and religious educators. Written for children age 5-11, but adaptable for all ages, *I Came From Joy!* offers fun and uplifting exercises that teach children values such as kindness, love, concentration, happiness, discrimination, sharing, patience, security, and how to be a success.

This easy-to-use workbook features: a complete curriculum for use at home, youth groups, schools, and Sunday schools; 26 lesson plans with all necessary materials; reproducible picture pages for coloring, arts and crafts, and bulletin boards; and much more.

GLOBAL KITCHEN
A Cookbook of Vegetarian Favorites from The Expanding Light Retreat
Diksha McCord

Create healthy, flavorful meals with an international flair! The delicious, easy-to-prepare recipes in *Global Kitchen* are inspired by many of the world's most-enjoyed culinary cultures—Italian, Thai, Indian, and Chinese, among others.

Blanche Agassy McCord was the head chef at The Expanding Light retreat for seven years, where she now teaches vegetarian cooking classes. She learned Kosher and vegetarian cooking while growing up in Israel, studied Japanese cooking while living in Kyoto, Japan, and learned Ayurvedic and Indian cooking from premier California chefs.

SIMPLY VEGETARIAN
Easy-to-Prepare Recipes for the Vegetarian Gourmet
Nancy Mair

Gourmet easy-to-prepare vegetarian dishes! A winning combination that includes 50 main dishes as well as a whole selection of soups, salads, and stunning desserts for a complete meal. This cookbook appeals to everyone, both vegetarian and non-vegetarian, whether family or guests. Completely revised, new recipes reflect the most current trends in gourmet cooking.

In this age of greater awareness about the need for more balance in our diet, *Simply Vegetarian!* offers meatless meals of superior taste. Easy-to-find ingredients and reasonable preparation times accommodate the schedule of the busiest cooks. The dishes, rich in taste and texture, please even the most sophisticated palate.

VEGETARIAN COOKING FOR STARTERS
Simple Recipes & Techniques for Health and Vitality
Diksha McCord

Are you confused by the many different foods, theories, fads, and techniques championed by various proponents of healthy eating? This book gives straightforward, easy-to-follow dietary advice, explains what common vegetarian foods are, offers useful explanations on how to prepare vegetarian dishes, and includes simple, savory recipes that will help you add vegetarian meals to your diet.

Most importantly, these low-fat recipes are delicious! So whether you'd like to become a complete vegetarian, incorporate some vegetarian eating into your current diet, or just learn how to cook vegetarian food for a loved one, this book is for you.

JOSEPH BHARAT CORNELL has helped people experience inner peace through his meditation and nature awareness work for thirty years. He has written six "Sharing Nature" books that have been published in twenty foreign languages and have "sparked a worldwide revolution in nature education." Millions around the world have enjoyed his joyful and inspiring nature writings and workshops.

Crystal Clarity is pleased to announce that we will soon be publishing the following titles by Joseph Bharat:

THE SKY AND EARTH TOUCHED ME

Wild seashores and woodlands calm and refresh our spirits. Contact with nature enhances our wholeness and well-being. The powerful, compelling exercises in this book help readers immerse themselves fully in nature's joyful and healing presence. Read *The Sky and Earth Touched Me* in a garden, backyard, or park. Part One is designed for personal practice; Part Two can be shared with a friend or a group, exercises that will help you discover invaluable nature awareness principles.

LISTENING TO NATURE

This book is arranged as a monthly diary to be used over and over again. Each day's entry offers an inspiring quotation, and usually includes an activity or explanation to help you absorb the idea as a personal experience. You can do these exercises anywhere, not necessarily outdoors. As you practice these activities more and more, you'll find your receptivity increasing, and you'll begin to see beauty all around you, even in the most common, everyday things.

THE BEST OF SHARING NATURE

Sharing Nature with Children, selling more than half a million copies, sparked a revolution in nature education all over the world. Now rewritten with new activities and games—and combined with its sequel, *Sharing Nature with Children II*—this single volume will no doubt extend nature education even further. With new exercises and old favorites, like *Get to Know a Tree*, parents, educators, and nature lovers everywhere will be enthralled by this phenomenal teaching tool.

CRYSTAL HERMITAGE GARDENS
A Photographic Pilgrimage to the Spiritual
Heart of Ananda Village
Barbara Bingham

Crystal Hermitage was the Northern California home of Swami Kriyananda, spiritual teacher and direct disciple of Paramhansa Yogananda, (author of the beloved classic *Autobiography of a Yogi*). The scenic beauty and peaceful atmosphere of Crystal Hermitage Gardens are reflected in the photographs and quotations contained in this book. Whether you are a nature lover or a spiritual seeker, these images will speak to you, whispering tranquility and inspiration to your soul through lush foliage, sun-kissed flowers, and stately statues.

SPACE, LIGHT, AND HARMONY
The Story of Crystal Hermitage
Swami Kriyananda

An adventure in design, building, and living, this is the true story of the evolution of a home—from initial planning to interior decorating—that serves as a powerful metaphor for personal development.

Years ago, the author withdrew to the woods in a personal search for clarity. In designing his home, he felt that it must reflect this inner search. In the process of building, the author explores practical topics such as what a home should express, architectural choices, interior design, and how to select art for your home. He also discusses deeper principles behind these choices, such as the importance of myth, the meaning of friendship, and the need to find balance in our lives. With over 70 beautiful full-color photographs, presented in gift-book format, this is the perfect present for all home owners.

THE SPIRIT OF GARDENING
Nancy Mair

A garden is about much more than just planting and watering. It can be, above all, a wonderful channel for your love, imagination, and attunement to nature. If you want to give more balance and harmony to your life, and nurture your spirit, this beautiful book will help transform your landscape . . . and your life. With in-depth explanations about visual style, color coordination, walkway construction, and overall garden design, it includes eye-catching full-color photography to provide inspiration to beginning and accomplished gardeners everywhere.

*The original 1946 unedited edition
of Yogananda's spiritual masterpiece*

AUTOBIOGRAPHY OF A YOGI
Paramhansa Yogananda

Autobiography of a Yogi is one of the best-selling Eastern philosophy titles of all time, with millions of copies sold, named one of the best and most influential books of the twentieth century. This highly prized reprinting of the original 1946 edition is the only one available free from textual changes made after Yogananda's death. Yogananda was the first yoga master of India whose mission was to live and teach in the West. In this updated edition are bonus materials, including a last chapter that Yogananda wrote in 1951, without posthumous changes.

THE NEW PATH
My Life with Paramhansa Yogananda
Swami Kriyananda

Winner of the 2010 Eric Hoffer Award for Best Self-Help/Spiritual Book
Winner of the 2010 USA Book News Award for Best Spiritual Book

This is the moving story of Kriyananda's years with Paramhansa Yogananda, India's emissary to the West and the first yoga master to spend the greater part of his life in America. When Swami Kriyananda discovered *Autobiography of a Yogi* in 1948, he was totally new to Eastern teachings. This is a great advantage to the Western reader, since Kriyananda walks us along the yogic path as he discovers it from the moment of his initiation as a disciple of Yogananda. With winning honesty, humor, and deep insight, he shares his journey on the spiritual path through personal stories and experiences.

THE ESSENCE OF THE BHAGAVAD GITA
Explained by Paramhansa Yogananda
Swami Kriyananda

This revelation approaches India's best-loved scripture from a fresh perspective, showing its deep allegorical meaning and its down-to-earth practicality. The themes presented are universal: how to achieve victory in life in union with the divine; how to prepare for life's "final exam," death, and what happens afterward; and how to triumph over all pain and suffering.